THE DIGESTIVE SYSTEM

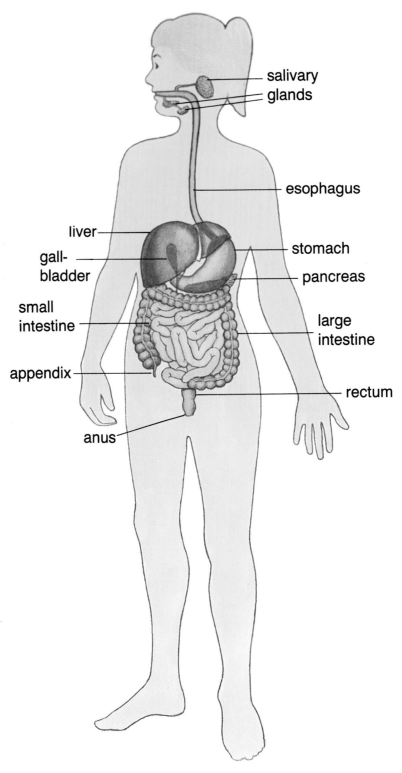

salivary
glands

esophagus

liver

gall-
bladder

stomach

pancreas

small
intestine

large
intestine

appendix

rectum

anus

The Digestive System

HUMAN
BODY
SYSTEMS

THE
DIGESTIVE
SYSTEM

BY DR. ALVIN, VIRGINIA, & ROBERT SILVERSTEIN

TWENTY–FIRST CENTURY BOOKS

A Division of Henry Holt and Company
New York

Twenty–First Century Books
A Division of Henry Holt and Company, Inc.
115 West 18th Street
New York, NY 10011

Henry Holt ® and colophon are trademarks of
Henry Holt and Company, Inc.
Publishers since 1866

Published in Canada by Fitzhenry & Whiteside Ltd.
195 Allstate Parkway, Markham, Ontario L3R 4T8

Library of Congress Cataloging-in-Publication Data
Silverstein, Alvin.
Digestive system / Alvin, Virginia, and Robert Silverstein. — 1st ed.
p. cm. — (Human body systems)
Includes index.
1. Digestive organs—Juvenile literature. [1. Digestive system.] I. Silverstein, Virginia B. II.
Silverstein, Robert A. III. Title. IV. Series.
QP145.S497 1994
612.3—dc20
94–19384
CIP
AC

First Edition 1994

Printed in Mexico
ISBN 0–8050–2832–3
All first editions are printed on acid–free paper ∞.
10 9 8 7 6 5 4 3 2 1

Drawings by Lloyd Birmingham

Photo Credits

Cover: Howard Sochurek/The Stock Market

pp. 9, 18, 19, 63, and 77: USDA; p. 10: Richard T. Nowitz/Photo Researchers, Inc.; p. 14: North Wind Pictures; p. 15: James Schnepf/The Gamma Liaison Network; p. 16: National Library of Medicine/Mark Marten/Photo Researchers, Inc.; p. 17: Novosti/Science Photo Library/Photo Researchers, Inc.; p. 24: David M. Grossman/Photo Researchers, Inc.; p. 25: Junebug Clark/Photo Researchers, Inc.; p. 28: Mark Newman/Photo Researchers, Inc.; p. 29: Tom McHugh/Photo Researchers, Inc.; p. 41: Fred Winner/Photo Researchers, Inc.; p. 47: Martin M. Rotker/Science Source/Photo Researchers, Inc.; p. 55: Richard Pasley/Liaison International; p. 65: Richard Hutchings/Photo Researchers, Inc.; p. 67: Biophoto Associates/Science Source/Photo Researchers, Inc.; pp. 68, 69: Renato Rotolo/Gamma Liaison; p. 75: NCI/Science Source/Photo Researchers, Inc.

CONTENTS

SECTION 1

FOOD FOR LIFE

What is your favorite food? A hot fudge sundae? French fries? Pizza? Tacos? Just thinking about these tasty foods, you may find that your mouth is beginning to water. This is the first step in a long series of processes that the body uses to break down the foods we eat. From them we get energy and new building materials.

Our bodies need energy for everything we do. We use energy when we run a race, watch TV, or even sleep. Energy is needed so that our muscles can contract, our heart can beat, and our lungs can breathe. We need new building materials in order to grow, and to replace worn-out or injured body parts. These building blocks are chemicals called **nutrients**.

Foods have to go through some big changes before our bodies can use the nutrients they contain. Even the tiniest crumb is too big to fit into our cells. And the chemicals in food are often too complex for the body to handle. Usually they must be broken down into simpler building blocks. The process of breaking down foods into smaller bits that can be used by the body is called **digestion**.

All living things must digest their food before they can get nourishment from it. Some creatures have simple ways of digesting food. Others, like humans, have a complicated digestive system to help break down foods and absorb nutrients into the body. Our digestive system is made up of a long passageway called the **digestive tract**, or **gut**, which stretches from the mouth to the anus, and several organs that help out in the process of digestion.

You are what you eat is an old but true saying. The average person eats half a ton of food each year. What did you eat yesterday? It may be hard to believe that the bowl of cereal you had for breakfast, the tuna sandwich you had for lunch, your spaghetti-and-meatball dinner, and the snacks and drinks you had during the day are now part of you. But the foods you eat are broken down into simple building blocks that your body uses to replace worn-out body parts. So, in a way, you really are what you eat.

HOW LIVING THINGS GET FOOD

Animals have to eat to get food, but plants don't. Green plants can make roots, leaves, and flowers out of nonliving substances. They turn water, carbon dioxide from the air, and minerals from the ground into **organic materials** (the chemicals of living organisms), using energy from sunlight to power their chemical reactions.

All other living creatures need the organic materials that plants create. They can get them either by eating plants or by eating animals that ate plants. Some animals, such as cows, horses, and rabbits, eat only plants. They are called **herbivores** (which means "grass eaters"). Other animals, such as lions and wolves, are called **carnivores** ("meat eaters"), because they eat only other animals. Humans are **omnivores** (meaning "eaters of everything"); they eat both plants and animals. The living creatures of the earth are thus linked together in complex **food chains**, each one feeding on others farther down the chain.

Corn is one of the world's most important crops. It has been used for food for about 10,000 years. Here a scientist checks a test crop of hybrid corn developed to resist disease.

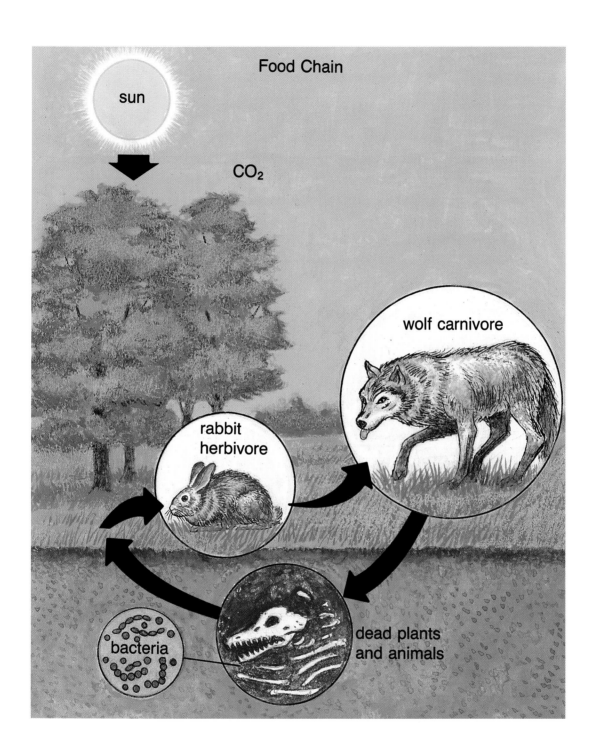

Food Chain

sun

CO_2

rabbit
herbivore

wolf carnivore

bacteria

dead plants
and animals

Some creatures are so tiny that their whole body consists of just a single cell. They take in food materials from the water in which they live and may not need any special digestive system. The ameba, for example, is a single-celled pond creature with a jellylike body. It wraps itself around its prey, which becomes trapped inside a tiny bubble called a food vacuole. There strong chemicals break food down into nutrients the ameba can use. But another single-celled animal, the paramecium, has some special structures for getting and digesting food: a mouth opening leads into a gullet, which is something like our throat. The gullet is lined with tiny hairlike structures called cilia, which wave back and forth to draw water inside. The water carries tiny creatures down the gullet into a food vacuole where chemicals digest the prey.

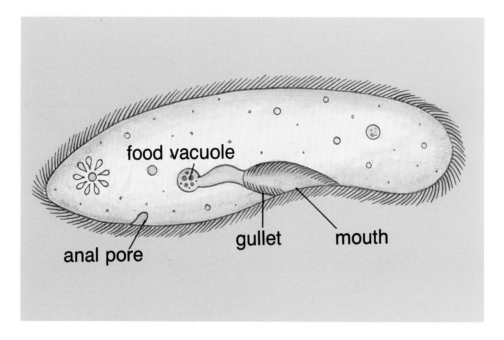

*The digestive system of a single-celled paramecium has
a few parts similar to the human digestive system.*

In lower animals food is often digested inside cells. But in more complicated animals, from earthworms up to humans, digestion takes place in a tube (the digestive tract, or gut) that runs through the body. Food enters at one end and passes down the digestive tract until the undigested materials pass out the other end. At a series of "service stations" along the tract, special organs work on the food, gradually breaking it down into usable bits.

GUTLESS PARASITES

Some parasites that live inside other animals are made up of many cells but do not have a gut. Tapeworms, for example, can grow inside an animal's digestive tract. They absorb nutrients through their body walls.

FOOD FOR HUMANS

Animals spend a lot of time eating or looking for food. Horses and cows graze on grass for hours. Field mice eat their weight in grass every day. The giant panda spends half the day eating bamboo shoots.

Today humans just pick out the foods they like at a store, and we spend relatively little time actually eating. But thousands of years ago, people's lives revolved around food. Early humans traveled from one place to another, hunting wild animals and picking fruits and vegetables. When they could not find any more to eat, they moved on to a new place.

Eventually people realized that they could plant seeds and grow crops. Wild animals were also caught and tamed. Some were used for meat; others provided milk to drink, or wool and hides to make clothing. Growing their own food allowed the early humans to settle down in permanent homes.

Before humans learned to plant they had to travel from place to place to find enough to eat.

When some people began to live in cities, the farmers had to grow extra food to feed the city dwellers, too. Machines were invented to help farmers grow more food with less work. Fertilizers, which contain the chemicals plants need to grow, helped farmers grow better harvests.

Better ways were also found to store food so that it could be transported many miles without spoiling. Food spoils when bacteria break it down. But drying food or salting it keeps it from spoiling. Pickling foods in vinegar also preserves them. And the low temperatures in a refrigerator or freezer help to keep bacteria from growing. One of the newest ways of keeping food from spoiling is irradiation. A brief exposure to radiation can kill bacteria without damaging the food. But many people are concerned about the safety of this method.

A lot of the food we eat today has been processed. In factories, foods like soups and cookies are prepared and cooked before they are packaged in boxes, sealed in cans, or frozen in airtight containers.

The packaging line at a food processing plant

Americans have many different foods to choose from. But many people around the world depend on just a few "staple" foods to supply their nutrients and provide energy. Rice is the staple food for nearly half the world; a third of the world relies on wheat. Other food staples are potatoes, corn, and cassavas.

THE FIRST COOKS

Prehistoric cave dwellers discovered fire and began cooking food. Cooking not only made food taste better, it also made it easier to digest. Heating is one way to break down fibers in meat and cellulose in plants. (Humans can't digest the cellulose fibers in plants, but cooking frees more of the starches and other nutrients trapped inside the plant cells than just chewing the food can release.)

DISCOVERING OUR DIGESTIVE SYSTEM

Ancient Egyptian doctors knew a lot about the gut and how it worked. Their records from more than **3,500** years ago contain treatments for digestive system problems. The ancient Greeks named the tube that brings food to the stomach the esophagus, which comes from words meaning "to carry away what is eaten."

Of course, not all of the old ideas about the digestive system were correct. Galen, a second-century Greek physician, helped to shape medical thinking for nearly 1,500 years. Galen suggested that food was carried from the gut to the liver, where it was changed into blood and joined with the spirit of life that flows inside us.

In the seventeenth century, scientists finally began to question Galen's ideas. But until the early 1700s, doctors believed that food just stayed in the stomach until it decayed. At that time scientists first began to understand a little about the changes in food that take place during digestion. The eighteenth-century French naturalist René de Réaumur, for example, showed that digestive juices in his pet bird's stomach helped break down food.

One of the greatest leaps in our understanding of the diges-

Galen

tive system occurred after a tragic accident. In 1822 a young Canadian soldier accidentally shot himself in the stomach. Dr. William Beaumont, an American army surgeon, was able to save the soldier's life, but the 2½-inch hole in his stomach wouldn't heal. When the hole was plugged up with bandages the soldier was able to eat and digest his food properly. Dr. Beaumont spent the next eight years observing how the stomach works. He made more than fifty discoveries about the stomach by observing through what is now called "Beaumont's window."

During the rest of the nineteenth century, other scientists discovered several special chemicals called **enzymes** that help to break down foods in the body.

In 1904 the Russian scientist Ivan Pavlov won a Nobel Prize for his discoveries about the digestive secretions of the stomach and the salivary glands in the mouth. In one of his famous experiments, Pavlov showed that dogs begin secreting digestive juices when they smell food or even anticipate a meal.

During this century, researchers learned much more about our digestive system. Modern technology has helped scientists treat many digestive problems. Scientists have even learned more about our digestive system by observing how digestion occurs in astronauts in the weightlessness of space.

Ivan Pavlov

THE FOODS WE EAT

There are many kinds of foods that we can eat to get the nutrients we need. Most foods contain several different nutrients. Food is really just tasty packaging, and the body has to break it down to separate out the nutrients it needs.

We enjoy a wide variety of foods such as meats, fruits, vegetables, and cheeses

Carbohydrates are the body's main source of energy. There are two types of carbohydrates. Starchy foods—such as bread, pasta, potatoes, and rice—usually contain many other nutrients the body needs. But sugary foods like soda and candies usually have very few other nutrients. Starches are broken down inside the body into a simple sugar called glucose. Glucose is the fuel needed by the body cells.

Proteins can also be used for energy, but they have another important use. They are the main building materials in the body. There are about 100,000 different kinds of proteins. They are found in your bones, hair, muscles, and skin. While you are growing, you need to eat a lot of protein, but even adults need it to replace worn-out body parts. Proteins are made up of smaller building blocks called amino acids. The proteins that we eat in meats, cheese, and eggs have to be broken down into amino acids so that the body can rearrange them into human proteins.

Fats are found in butter, cheese, margarine, oil, and meat, and most people know that too much fat is not good for us. But the body does need a certain amount—fats are used in the cell membrane of every cell in our body, for example. Fats can also be broken down and used for energy. Extra fat is stored in the body.

Vitamins and minerals are not used for energy, but they are needed in tiny amounts to help keep us healthy. Minerals like calcium help to strengthen our teeth and bones; iron helps the blood carry oxygen to the body cells. Vitamins help the body to get energy from food. They also have many other uses. Vitamin K, for example, helps you stop bleeding when you get a cut, and vitamin D helps build bones and teeth. Eating the proper foods usually supplies all the vitamins and minerals we need.

The tough part of vegetables, grains, and fruits that the body cannot digest is called fiber. Fiber is important because it adds bulk to the food in our digestive tract and helps keep it moving along smoothly.

Water is one of the most important nutrients. Almost everything that goes on in our bodies involves water. Three-quarters of the body's weight is made up of water. We drink only half the water that our body needs. We get the rest from food. Crackers are pretty dry, but they are 5 percent water. Cucumbers seem pretty juicy, and they are— 98 percent water!

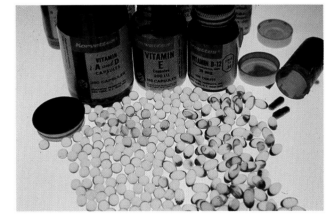

Vitamin pills can be an important supplement, but eating a balanced diet is the best way to get necessary vitamins and minerals.

SECTION 2

OUR DIGESTIVE SYSTEM

Our digestive system is like a "disassembly line." Food enters at the mouth, where it is cut and ground into smaller pieces. These pieces are slowly broken down as the food travels through a long tube called the gut. The food is mixed and mashed and broken down with chemicals called enzymes until it is converted to forms the body can use. Nutrients are absorbed by the body, but unusable materials are excreted out the **anus,** the opening at the other end of the gut.

It sounds strange, but food in the digestive tract is not really "inside" the body. The gut is just a tube inside us that is open at both ends. The tube bulges in some places and is pinched in at others. Amazingly, the gut is from 20 to 30 feet long, or about 6 to 9 meters (depending on how old and how large a person is). It is coiled to fit inside your body.

The digestion of food starts in the mouth. Your **teeth** chew it into small pieces, and enzymes in your **saliva** start breaking down some of the food materials. The food is then swallowed down the **esophagus,** or **gullet,** into the baglike **stomach.** After being mixed with more chemicals, it passes into a long, thin, coiled tube called the **small intestine.**

The **pancreas** and the **liver** supply the digestive system with digestive juices to break down the food. Inside the small intestine, enzymes break down most of the food into a liquid. Nutrients are absorbed through the walls of the small intestine into the bloodstream and are delivered to the body cells.

The food that cannot be digested continues on into a short, but wide, coiled tube called the **large intestine.** Extra liquid is removed, and the undigested food material leaves your body as **feces.**

The structure of the digestive system is very similar throughout the gut. It is made up of several layers. In some parts of the gut, particular lay-

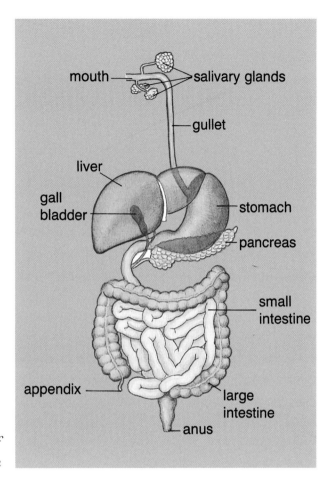

*The main parts of
the digestive system*

ers are thicker or thinner depending on the job that needs to be done in that part of the digestive tract.

The outermost layer of the gut is called the **serosa**. It protects the gut and keeps it moist so that it can move around inside the body. Beneath this layer are two layers of muscles that help move food along the digestive tract. The muscles are wrapped around the **submucosa**. This sturdy but elastic layer gives the gut its shape. It contains blood vessels that deliver the nutrients the digestive system needs to keep working properly. It also contains nerves that help control the muscles of the gut. The innermost layer is called the **mucosa**. Glands in this layer secrete enzymes or a thick liquid called **mucus**. The mucosa is coated with mucus to protect the tract from chemicals that break down food and from germs that might be in food.

ARE YOU HUNGRY?

Picture a juicy peach, a hamburger on a bun, or some other food you enjoy. If you haven't eaten in a while, thinking about these foods may be making you hungry. Eating is so much a part of our daily lives that often just the sight of food or the thought of eating can make us start to feel hungry.

For most people, hunger is not a very pleasant feeling. When babies are hungry, they cry. When you get hungry your stomach may begin to feel a little "empty." If you can't eat right away, you may feel your stomach contracting, which sends out hunger pains. When you get really hungry you may feel grouchy and irritable. You may not be able to concentrate or think clearly. These are important signals your body is sending you. It is telling you that it's time to eat—the trillions of cells that make up your body need nourishment.

Before you even start eating, your digestive system starts getting ready. Digestive juices begin to flow in preparation for the food you are about to eat. This happens without your even knowing it. But how does the body know when to expect a meal?

Most people usually eat at regular times during the day. The body gets used to this pattern. So if you're used to eating lunch at noon and one day you have to wait until later, chances are you will feel hungry. Has your stomach ever started growling just when everyone in

A baby's hunger cry demands immediate attention.

class was quiet? Your stomach was pouring out digestive juices and churning them around like a washing machine because it was expecting food.

When you smell something delicious cooking, your brain may start sending hunger messages to get you ready to eat. It also sends messages to start the digestive process.

How foods smell tells us what tastes we can expect. Humans can tell the difference among hundreds of different food smells. Smells can also tell us when food is spoiled, warning us not to eat it. The way foods look can also give us clues about how they will taste.

When we do things that use energy—like playing a rough game of football on a cold day—hunger feelings prompt us to eat and restock the body's fuel supply. Exercise uses a lot of energy. So does keeping the body at the right temperature when it is cold outside.

Ideally, we get hungry when our bodies need nutrients. Unfortunately, this doesn't always work properly. When we're sick, we may lose our

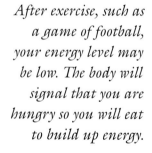

After exercise, such as a game of football, your energy level may be low. The body will signal that you are hungry so you will eat to build up energy.

appetite, even though more nutrients than usual are needed. And we often eat when we're not really hungry. Some people eat when they are nervous or depressed. Many people eat while they are watching television, without thinking about what or how much they are snacking. And people who get into the habit of eating too much may feel hungry when their bodies really don't need more food.

TAKE A BITE

Digestion starts in the mouth when we take a bite of food. Some foods are hard, but some are soft and squishy. Our mouths can handle all kinds of foods. Our teeth break up foods that are too big to swallow.

Humans can eat a wider variety of foods than most other animals because we have four different kinds of teeth. The sharp, chisel-shaped **incisors** in the front act like knives to slice and bite off chunks of food. Next to the incisors are the **canines**. They are pointed to tear the food into bits. Farther back are the **premolars** and the **molars**. These are flat with raised bumps and ridges to crush and grind food into a smooth pulp.

Our jaw muscles let our teeth grind up food with great force. For their size, jaw muscles are probably the most powerful muscles in the body. They help the teeth chew food to a pulp in seconds.

Humans have two sets of teeth. A child has 20 "milk teeth." At an age of about five or six, these baby teeth start to fall out and are replaced by 32 permanent teeth.

The whitish covering on the teeth is **enamel**, the hardest substance in the body. It protects the inner layers of the tooth. Beneath the enamel is a softer, yellow, bonelike cushioning layer called **dentin**. The center of the tooth is the soft **pulp**, which contains blood vessels and nerves. The teeth are firmly held in the jawbone by roots.

The ancient Egyptians thought we got toothaches because the gods were upset with us. Today we know that cavities occur when bacteria turn sugar and other carbohydrates into an acid that eats away at the enamel. If the acid makes a small hole, bacteria can get inside to the softer layers and cause problems. Brushing our teeth and flossing after meals helps remove

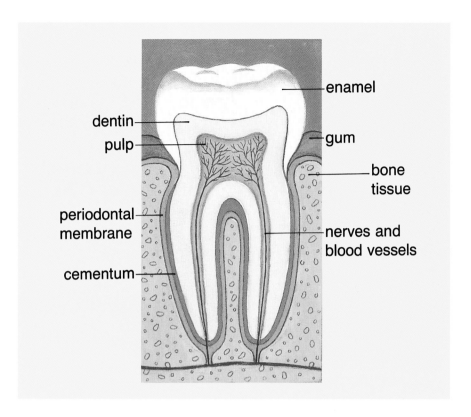

The basic structure of a molar

a thin, sticky film called plaque that contains bacteria and food particles. Seeing a dentist regularly is important, too, so that the teeth can be thoroughly cleaned and cavities can be filled while they are still small. Fluoride in toothpaste protects teeth by helping to strengthen the enamel.

When you are reminded to chew your food thoroughly, this is really good advice. Food can pass through the digestive tract more easily when it

DID YOU KNOW . . .

Your front teeth can bite into foods with a force of 55 pounds. Your back molars can grind foods with a force of 200 pounds.

This lioness has teeth well adapted to tearing apart large chunks of meat. It does very little chewing before swallowing the chunks.

is ground up into smaller particles, and digestive juices can do their job better. Doctors believe that some digestive problems are caused by eating too quickly. Carnivores rip off pieces of meat and swallow them whole. But their digestive system is equipped to handle large solid chunks of food. Seals swallow stones that stay in their stomachs to help grind food. So do birds, which have no teeth at all.

When a shark's teeth get worn down,
new teeth move in to replace them.

MOUTH-WATERING MEAL

Each day as much as six cups of spit, or saliva, is produced in your mouth. That may sound like a lot, but saliva is very important.

The mouth and throat are kept moist by a slow but continuous flow of saliva. Extra saliva is produced when we eat. Smelling, seeing, or even thinking about food is enough to start it flowing. Saliva helps to soften and moisten even the driest foods. The tongue mixes food with saliva as it pushes the food around the mouth, mashing it against the roof of the mouth and against the teeth so that we can chew thoroughly.

It would be very hard to swallow anything without saliva. It helps the tongue shape the chewed-up food into a ball, or **bolus**, which is then sent to the back of the mouth to be swallowed. Mucus in the saliva coats the bolus so that it will slide easily down the esophagus.

Saliva helps in other ways, too. It helps to cool down or warm up food to a comfortable temperature. Saliva helps us to taste foods. It also keeps the mouth healthy. It washes away bacteria and bits of food, and it kills some bacteria. Enzymes in saliva also start breaking down complex carbohydrates into simple sugars.

Saliva is produced by three main pairs of **salivary glands** in the mouth. The smallest pair, the **sublingual glands**, are under the tongue, the **submaxillary glands** are in the lower jaw, and the largest pair, the **parotid glands**, are just below the ears. Saliva flows through tiny tubes into the mouth. Other cells in the cheeks and on your tongue also add to the liquid in your mouth.

A REACTION YOU CAN TASTE

If you keep chewing on a cracker, after a while it will start to taste sweet. This is because an enzyme in saliva called ptyalin has started to break down starch into sugars.

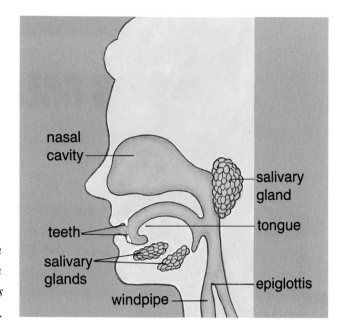

Digestion starts in the mouth when you chew food and it is mixed with saliva.

nasal cavity

salivary gland

teeth

tongue

salivary glands

epiglottis

windpipe

Saliva is more than 99 percent water. It can be thin and watery or thick and full of mucus. The amount and composition of saliva are influenced by what foods we are eating. You salivate more when you see or smell foods you like. Sour-tasting foods and dry or hard foods also cause more saliva to be produced. But bitter foods stimulate thicker saliva.

TASTES GREAT

What are your favorite foods? Chocolate ice cream? Ripe cherries? A juicy steak? Each person has a different list, but we all decide which foods we like or dislike according to how they taste.

Taste is a chemical sense. Chemicals from foods dissolve in the saliva in your mouth and are carried to special taste receptor cells on the surface of the tongue. They send messages along nerves to taste centers in the brain. There the taste sensations are sorted out.

If you look at your tongue in the mirror, you'll find that it has a rough and pebbly surface. Under a microscope, the bumps on the surface of the tongue, called **papillae**, look like little roses or cabbage heads, tiny leaves, or (toward the back of the tongue) small doughnuts. These papillae con-

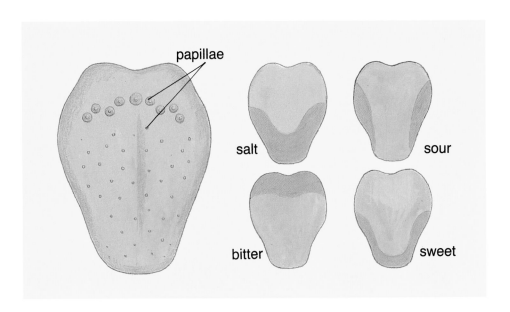

Taste bud areas on the tongue

tain **taste buds**, which are sensitive to particular kinds of food chemicals. An adult has about 10,000 taste buds. You can distinguish hundreds of different tastes, but there are only four kinds of taste buds. Each kind responds to a particular taste: sweet, sour, salty, or bitter.

The taste buds of each kind are grouped together. Those sensitive to sweet tastes are found in the front of the tongue (the first part that dips into a mouthful of food or liquid). The taste buds for salty and sour tastes are on the sides of the tongue. And bitter tastes are picked up by taste buds at the back of the tongue.

Most foods stimulate more than one kind of taste bud. The flavors of foods are blends of the four primary tastes. Some foods taste sweet when you first taste them but bitter as they go down into the throat.

Most people like sweet tastes and dislike very bitter tastes. We use our taste sense to judge whether foods are good to eat. (A bitter taste can be a useful warning because some deadly poisons produced by plants taste bitter.) Our heredity helps to determine how things taste to us. Some people are more sensitive to bitter tastes than others, for example. Our reactions to tastes are formed by our past experiences with foods. People can learn to like tastes and food textures they disliked at first.

Our sense of smell contributes to the taste of foods. That is why everything tastes "blah" when your nose is stuffed up by a cold.

MAPPING YOUR TONGUE

Fill four glasses halfway with water. Stir a teaspoon of sugar into one glass, a teaspoon of salt into the second, a teaspoon of vinegar into the third, and a teaspoon of instant coffee into the fourth. Wipe your tongue dry with a clean cloth, and then moisten a cotton swab with the sugar solution and touch it to various parts of your tongue. Sketch the outline of your tongue on a piece of paper and mark the places where you felt a sweet taste. Wipe your tongue again and repeat the test, using a new cotton swab each time, with the salt, vinegar, and coffee solutions to map the salty, sour, and bitter tastes.

SECTION 3

SWALLOWING FOOD

Digestion has barely begun when food is ready to leave the mouth. The teeth and saliva have changed it into a soft, mushy mass, which the tongue has shaped into a rough ball (the bolus). Enzymes are breaking down some of the food starches into sugars. But no further digestion will occur until the bolus gets to the next "work station," the stomach. For that, it must be swallowed.

When you are ready to swallow a mouthful of food, your tongue pushes the bolus up and back—past the roof of the mouth (which consists of the **hard palate** in front and the **soft palate** toward the back) and finally into the throat, in the part called the **pharynx.** You can control the beginning of a swallow, but once food reaches the pharynx it is too late to change your mind. From that point on, swallowing is an automatic reflex action, and you can't stop even if you try to.

The pharynx is actually a double-duty tube. Food passes through it on the way down to the stomach, and air travels through it going to and from the lungs. Two "trap doors" work to keep the flows of food and air from getting mixed up. If you open your mouth wide and look at your throat in a mirror, you will see a U-shaped flap hanging down at the back of the soft palate. That is the **uvula.** When you swallow, it flaps upward and closes off the airway leading into the nose. Meanwhile, another flap, the **epiglottis,** folds over to cover the opening into the

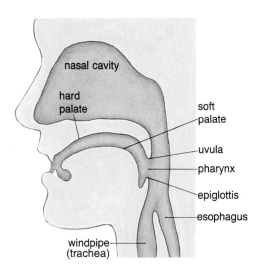

nasal cavity

hard
palate

soft
palate

uvula

pharynx

epiglottis

esophagus

windpipe
(trachea)

trachea, the air pipe leading down into the lungs. So the bolus is sent into the esophagus, the food pipe leading to the stomach.

Sometimes, especially if you talk or laugh while you are eating or drinking, the uvula may not work fast enough. Then bits of food or liquid squirt up into your nose. If the epiglottis does not close off the trachea quickly enough when you swallow, food "goes down the wrong way." You feel a painful lump in your throat, and you cough and sputter until the food is blown out of your trachea.

Swallowing a big mouthful of food that has not been chewed properly can be dangerous. A person can choke to death at the dinner table if a chunk of meat or some other solid food is accidentally swallowed into the trachea. Prompt first aid, by striking the person on the back or using the **Heimlich maneuver** (the "hug of life") to make the food plug pop out of the air pipe, can save a choking person's life.

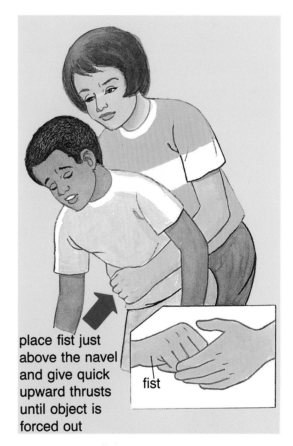

place fist just above the navel and give quick upward thrusts until object is forced out

fist

This illustration shows how to perform the Heimlich maneuver. It may take several thrusts to force out the plug of food blocking the windpipe.

DID YOU KNOW . . .

A person swallows an average of 3,000 times a day.

MOVING RIGHT ALONG

When you drink, the force of a swallow can usually send a mouthful of liquid straight down the esophagus into the stomach. But solid food (even though it is already rather soft and mushy) has to be pushed along.

When food enters the esophagus, circular muscles in its wall, just behind the bolus, contract. The tube gets narrower, pushing the food downward. Then the next ring of circular muscles contracts to force the food farther along. The contractions continue to move along, down the whole 10-inch (25-centimeter) length of the esophagus. The food is forced along, in much the same way that you squeeze toothpaste out of a tube.

At the end of the esophagus, the opening into the stomach is guarded

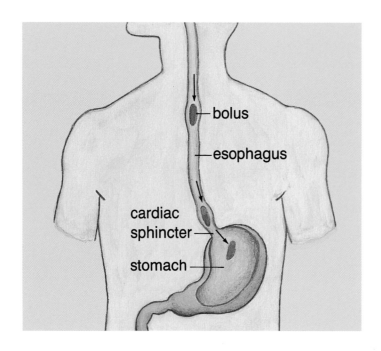

Solid food is pushed along by muscular contractions in the esophagus.

by a strong ring of muscle called the **cardiac sphincter**. (A sphincter is a ring-shaped muscle that draws in like a purse string. The *cardiac* part of the name comes from the fact that it is near the heart.) When the bolus reaches the end of the esophagus, the cardiac sphincter relaxes, widening the opening, and the food squirts into the stomach.

Gravity helps to send the food moving along, but the contractions of the esophagus are strong enough to work without or even against gravity. Astronauts in space have no trouble swallowing their food, and you could swallow while lying down or even while standing on your head.

The wavelike contractions that move down the esophagus are called **peristalsis**, and they occur in all parts of the digestive tract. They keep the food moving along, without backing up or clogging up the tract.

WHAT IS HEARTBURN?

Sometimes the cardiac sphincter does not stay closed tightly enough. Then acidic stomach contents may splash up into the esophagus, producing a burning pain in the middle of the chest. This is heartburn, which really has nothing to do with the heart. It can be caused by bending forward when the stomach is very full, or by eating foods such as chocolate or onions, which relax the cardiac sphincter. Emotional upsets around mealtimes can also cause heartburn. Antacids help ease the pain by neutralizing some of the stomach acid.

IN THE STOMACH

Do you know where your stomach is? Most people would point to the belly button. Actually, though, the stomach is at the top of the abdomen, just under the diaphragm, the sheet of muscle that forms the floor of the chest cavity. An empty stomach is shaped like a letter J, and its inner walls are drawn up into long, soft folds called **rugae**. As the stomach fills with food, it bulges out to the shape of a boxing glove and the rugae disappear. An average adult's stomach can hold as much as 2.5 pints (1.4 liters) of food.

Powerful muscles form most of the stomach wall. The stomach muscles contract, mixing and churning the stomach contents. The contractions occur in a regular rhythm, usually about three per minute. Emotions such as anger or fear can speed up the contractions and make them stronger.

Special cells in the stomach lining act as tiny glands, pouring their secretions into the churning mass of food. One of them, **hydrochloric acid**, helps to soften food and also kills any germs it might contain. Another stomach secretion, **pepsinogen**, is

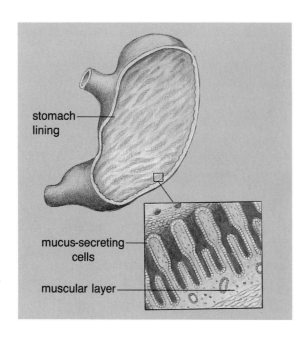

stomach lining

mucus-secreting cells

muscular layer

A layer of mucus in the lining protects the stomach from being digested by its strong secretions.

changed by hydrochloric acid into a protein-digesting enzyme, pepsin. (In children, stomach cells also produce another enzyme, called **rennin**, which helps to digest milk.) Some stomach cells secrete **mucus**, a thick, gooey liquid that helps to moisten the food. Together the stomach secretions are called **gastric juice**.

The hydrochloric acid produced by the stomach glands is strong enough to burn a hole in a carpet or dissolve the iron in a nail. Why doesn't it digest the stomach itself? The delicate cells in the stomach lining are protected by a coating of mucus. Even so, the lining cells wear out quickly and are constantly being replaced by new ones. In fact, the whole stomach lining is replaced every three days.

In about three to six hours the food in the stomach is churned into a soupy liquid called **chyme**. Some simple food chemicals and drugs, including sugar, alcohol, and aspirin, are also absorbed through the stomach wall into the bloodstream. Peristalsis moves the rest of the food downward. With each wave of contractions the **pyloric sphincter**, the muscle guarding the exit from the stomach, opens and allows a bit of chyme to squirt out into the intestines.

WHAT CAUSES BURPS?

You swallow some air when you eat or drink, especially if you eat too quickly. Gases may also be formed when food is digested. And carbonated drinks contain a lot of gas under high pressure. As the gases build up, the pressure inside the stomach increases. From time to time the cardiac sphincter pops open, and a burst of gas explodes up into the esophagus.

DID YOU KNOW . . .

A starfish pushes its stomach out through its mouth and squeezes it into a clamshell to digest its meal.

A cow has four stomachs to help it digest plant fibers.

A starfish uses its powerful tentacles to force open a clamshell.

DIGESTION IN THE SMALL INTESTINE

When you have a "stomachache," the pain you feel is probably coming from your intestines. Together the small and large intestines take up most of the space inside the abdomen. The small intestine alone is about 20 feet (6 meters) long. This long, thin tube is looped and coiled to fit inside the abdominal cavity.

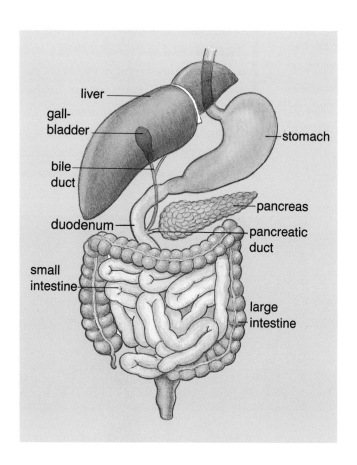

liver

gall-
bladder

bile
duct

duodenum

small
intestine

stomach

pancreas

pancreatic
duct

large
intestine

Chyme from the stomach squirts into the first part of the small intestine, called the **duodenum**. It is about 10 inches (25 centimeters) long and is shaped like a letter C. After the duodenum, the small intestine continues for 8 or 9 feet (2.4 or 2.7 meters) as the **jejunum**, and then for another 10 feet (3 meters) or so as the **ileum**.

The main work of digestion occurs in the duodenum and jejunum. When chyme squirts into the duodenum, cells in the intestinal lining are stimulated to secrete **intestinal juice**. These secretions include mucus to protect the duodenal lining from the acid in the chyme and various enzymes for digesting proteins, carbohydrates, and fats.

Two other "juices" also pour into the duodenum, through small tubes (ducts) coming from nearby organs. The pancreas contributes **sodium bicarbonate**, which neutralizes the acid in the chyme, and some powerful digestive enzymes. **Bile**, formed in the liver, is stored temporarily in the gallbladder and then flows into the duodenum when there is food to be digested. Bile is not an enzyme, and it does not actually digest anything. But it helps in the digestion of fats by breaking down large globs of fat into tiny droplets that the fat-digesting enzymes can work on.

Normally it takes about five hours for the digestive enzymes to convert food materials into simple nutrients that the body can use. A very high-fat meal may take somewhat longer to digest.

Although a coating of mucus helps to protect the lining of the small intestine, the digestive enzymes are very hard on its delicate cells. They wear out quickly. On the average, they die off and are replaced by new lining cells after about 48 hours.

DIGESTION IN ACTION

Today's laundry detergents usually contain enzymes that get rid of stains by breaking down proteins and fats, in much the same way that the enzymes in the intestines digest food chemicals. Mix a tablespoon of detergent into a glass of warm water, then add a hard-boiled egg, cut into slices. Allow it to stand for a few days, checking the size and appearance of the egg slices each day. Egg white is almost pure protein, and the yolk is high in fat. What do your observations tell you about the enzymes in the detergent?

THE PANCREAS

The pancreas looks rather like a flattened pink fish, about 6 inches (15 centimeters) long. It lies behind the stomach, with its "head" resting in the curve of the duodenum and its "tail" touching the spleen. Its name comes from Greek words meaning "all meat," because it contains no bones or fat.

The pancreas is actually two organs in one. It produces **pancreatic juice**, a mixture of digestive enzymes and other substances that flow into the duodenum through the pancreatic duct. Scientists call an organ whose secretions are delivered by ducts to the place where they act an **exocrine gland**. Other exocrine glands in the body include the sweat glands in the skin, which help to cool the body, and the tear glands that keep the eyeballs moist (and sometimes overflow when you are unhappy). There are also a number of "ductless" or **endocrine glands**, whose secretions pass into the bloodstream and are carried by the blood to wherever they are needed. The pancreas is also an important endocrine gland. It produces **hormones**, chiefly **insulin** and **glucagon**, which control how much sugar the body uses for energy and how much is stored away for future use.

The endocrine parts of the pancreas are scattered like little islands through the organ, and they are named **islets of Langerhans**. Under a microscope the rest of the pancreas, which produces the digestive juices, looks like clusters of grapes, called **acini**. Cells in the acini pour secretions into microscopic ducts, which combine into larger ones. They all drain into the main **pancreatic duct**, which runs through the whole length of the pancreas, from head to tail, and empties into the duodenum.

The protein-digesting enzymes of the pancreas, trypsin and chymotrypsin, are so powerful that they could digest the organ itself. But, like

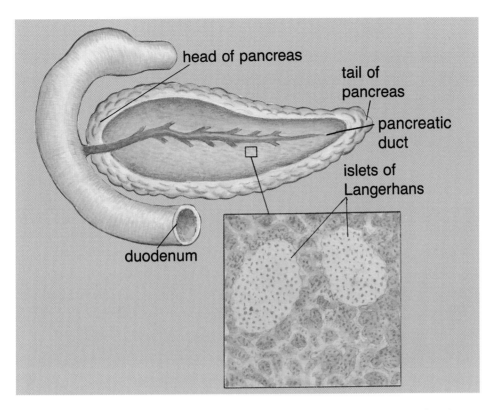

The pancreas acts as both a digestive organ and an endocrine gland.

the pepsin that works in the stomach, they are produced in inactive forms (trypsinogen and chymotrypsinogen), which are converted to the active enzymes in the small intestine. The digestive enzymes of the pancreas also include **amylase**, which converts starches to sugars, and **lipase**, which works with bile to break down fats into simpler building blocks—fatty acids and glycerol. The pancreas produces more secretions when food enters the duodenum. Its pancreatic juice contains just the right mix of ingredients to handle the job: enough sodium bicarbonate to neutralize the hydrochloric acid in the chyme, along with amounts of digestive enzymes to match the amounts of protein, carbohydrate, and fat in the meal.

As an endocrine gland, if the pancreas does not produce enough insulin, a person develops diabetes, a disease in which the blood sugar level is not controlled. Scientists now think Type I diabetes, which develops at an early age, may be caused by a virus that results in damage to the pancreas. If the virus can be identified, a vaccine could be developed to prevent Type I diabetes.

THE LIVER AND BILE

The liver is the largest organ of the body, weighing about 3 to 4 pounds (about 1.4 to 1.8 kilograms). It lies in the top of the abdominal cavity, tucked snugly under the diaphragm. It is a deep reddish brown color, and its surface seems to be smooth and rubbery. But this organ actually contains as many as 100,000 tiny units called **lobules**, each provided with drainage ducts and a rich blood supply.

The liver works as the body's chemical factory. More than 500 different functions have been discovered. It converts the sugar glucose to a starch form, **glycogen**; stores the glycogen; and then changes it back into glucose when the body needs more sugar. In fact, the **portal vein** carries most of the products of digestion to the liver, where they may be converted to other substances. It also stores vitamins and iron. The liver filters poisons and wastes out of the blood and converts them to less harmful chemicals. It manufactures blood proteins, blood-clotting chemicals, and cholesterol. And it produces bile, a greenish yellow liquid that drains through the bile ducts into the baglike gallbladder.

The liver makes 1 to 2 pints of bile each day. Normally the bile is stored in the gallbladder until there is fat-containing food to be digested. Then the

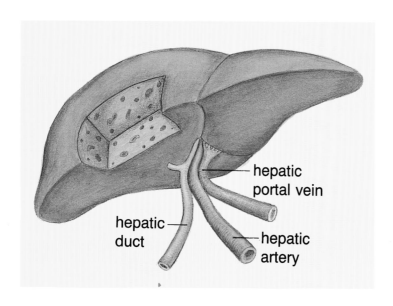

hepatic portal vein

hepatic duct

hepatic artery

stored bile is emptied into the duodenum, where it acts as an **emulsifying agent**, breaking down globs of fat into tiny droplets and helping to keep them suspended in the watery fluid in the digestive tract.

A person can live without a gallbladder if it becomes diseased and must be removed surgically. It is really just a temporary storage place. (Eating a low-fat diet allows the steady trickle of bile from the liver to handle the digestive load.) But no one can live without a liver. It does too many important things. Fortunately, the liver has an amazing ability to repair itself. If as much as 90 percent of the liver is removed, the small piece remaining can grow back into a full-sized organ. (In some diseases, such as cirrhosis of the liver in alcoholics or people with chronic hepatitis, the liver may become too damaged to repair itself.)

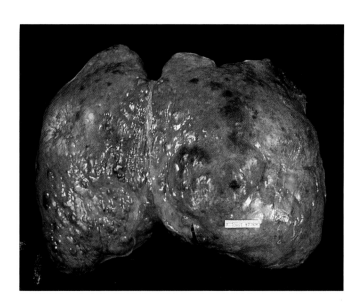

This photo shows scarring of the liver caused by cirrhosis.

SECTION 4

ABSORBING FOOD MATERIALS

The digestion of foods would not be of much use without some way of getting nutrients to the body cells. So the digestive tract also provides for the absorption of nutrients into the bloodstream. This occurs in the small intestine, especially in the jejunum and ileum.

It has been calculated that the inner lining of the small intestine has a total surface area of nearly 300 square yards—about the size of a tennis court. That seems like an enormous area to pack into a narrow tube, even if it is about 20 feet (6 meters) long. The extra area is provided by some unusual structures.

The inner lining of the small intestine is drawn into ridges and folds, and its surface looks like velvet. A microscope reveals that it is covered with millions of tiny, fingerlike structures called **villi**. The villi, in turn, are cov-

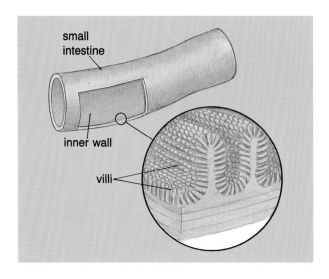

Millions of tiny villi line the small intestine and greatly increase the area of the small intestine where digestion occurs.

ered with even tinier **microvilli**, forming a fringe that scientists call the **brush border**. Together the folds, villi, and microvilli make the inner surface area about 600 times as great as it would be if the intestines were just smooth tubes.

Inside each finger-shaped **villus** there is a network of blood capillaries, surrounding a lymph vessel called a **lacteal**. The amino acids produced in protein digestion and the simple sugars obtained from more complex carbohydrates can pass right through the intestinal lining and the thin capillary walls. These nutrients are carried off by the blood flowing through the capillary network. This blood drains into veins that connect with the portal vein leading to the liver. Meanwhile, the fat nutrients pass into the lacteals. The contents of these lymph vessels eventually drain into the bloodstream and find their way to the liver.

While digestion and absorption are going on, peristaltic contractions churn and mix the intestinal contents and send them moving along. The villi also help by bending, waving, contracting, and straightening up again. Their movements also help to keep blood flowing through the capillary network.

TRANSPORTING FOOD

Thousands of chemical reactions are going on, right now, in your body cells. These reactions allow you to move, to breathe, and to think. They help to repair damaged tissues and organs, too. Blood and lymph carry the nutrients needed for all these reactions.

Large blood vessels called arteries carry oxygen-rich blood from the heart to all parts of the body. The arteries branch again and again, forming

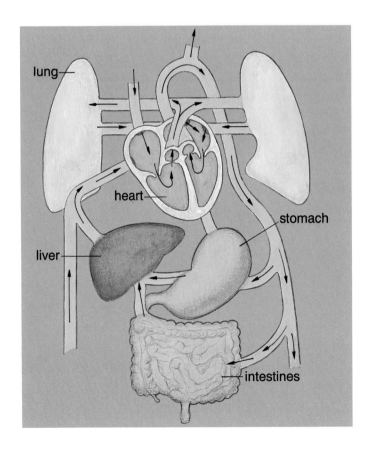

lung

heart

liver

stomach

intestines

This diagram shows the blood flow to and from the digestive system.

smaller and smaller blood vessels. The tiniest are the capillaries, which form networks reaching nearly all the body cells. Oxygen, needed to get energy from food, passes easily through the thin capillary walls and into the body cells. Carbon dioxide, which is produced when the cells use nutrients for energy, passes into the capillaries and is carried away in the blood. The capillaries merge into larger and larger blood vessels. The largest are the veins, which return blood to the heart.

The muscles in the stomach and intestinal walls have a rich blood supply, which brings them the energy and nutrients they need to keep up their contractions. The capillaries in the small intestine pick up cell waste products and also carry away the nutrients that are absorbed through the villi. They drain into the large portal vein, which goes to the liver. There the various nutrients are processed into different forms, and many of them are stored before the blood flows on to the veins leading to the heart.

The blood vessels that service the intestines and liver are wrapped in a large sheet of membrane called the mesentery. The mesentery also helps to hold the intestines in place in the abdominal cavity, keeping them from getting tangled as they wriggle about during peristalsis.

SIESTA TIME

While food is being digested and absorbed, the flow of blood to the digestive organs increases greatly. As much as 30 percent of the blood pumped by the heart flows through the intestines. So, while you are digesting a meal, there is less blood available for other body organs, such as the skeletal muscles and brain. That is why you may feel sleepy after a meal (your brain is not getting as much oxygen and nutrients) and why heavy exercise after eating may lead to painful cramps (the muscles are not getting enough blood supply to cope with the extra load). In some countries, a few hours in the afternoon—a siesta—are reserved for rest and digestion of the large midday meal.

CONTROLLING THE DIGESTIVE SYSTEM

What makes your stomach lining start secreting hydrochloric acid when there is food to be digested? How does the pancreas find out that its secretions are needed in the intestines? What makes you feel "full" when you have eaten enough food?

The body has two main ways of controlling and coordinating its many activities: by messages that travel along threadlike nerves and by chemical messengers called **hormones**. The main nerve involved in the work of the digestive system is the **vagus nerve**. Its name means "wanderer," and its branches ramble through much of the body. Starting at the lower part of the brain, it carries messages to the stomach, the small and large intestines, and key sphincter muscles such as the pyloric sphincter at the opening from the stomach into the duodenum and the anal sphincter at the very end of the large intestine. (Other branches of the vagus nerve go to the heart and the bladder.) Hormones also help to control digestion.

When food enters the stomach, sensory nerves pick up the stretching of the stomach walls and the contact of food chemicals with its lining. These signals are relayed up to the brain, then back along the vagus nerve to the stomach. The nerve messages prompt the tiny gland cells in the stomach lining to start secreting gastric juice. They also stimulate the production of a stomach hormone, **gastrin**, which makes the lining cells pour out hydrochloric acid. Sometimes just smelling, tasting, or even thinking about food is enough to start the process going, as messages are relayed down from the brain through the vagus nerve.

Some of the gastrin travels through the bloodstream to the pancreas. Together with messages from the vagus nerve, it prompts the pancreas to start secreting its digestive juices. The duodenum and jejunum secrete their own hormones, **cholecystokinin** and **secretin**, when chyme enters the small intestine. These hormones also signal gland cells in the pancreas and the intestinal lining to produce digestive juices. Cholecystokinin and vagus nerve messages also cause the gallbladder to contract and send bile into the duodenum.

A part of the brain called the **hypothalamus** contains special centers that keep track of various chemicals in the blood. As sugars, amino acids, and other digested nutrients enter the blood, the hypothalamus turns off the hunger messages. Meanwhile, nerves have been relaying the news that the stomach wall is getting stretched by a load of food and adding to the message that you are "full."

A technician points to the hypothalamus as it appears on a computer screen during an MRI scan of the brain.

Usually, unless you have eaten so much that your stretched-out stomach feels uncomfortable, you are not aware of any of these nerve and chemical messages. The control of digestion is an automatic process, which goes on without your thinking or even knowing about it.

GETTING RID OF WASTES

Our bodies cannot use everything in food. Fruits, vegetables, and grains, for example, contain a lot of **cellulose**, which is the main building block in the walls of plant cells. Cellulose is actually made up of many sugar molecules, chemically linked together. So is starch, an important food carbohydrate. Our digestive enzymes can split starch molecules, to free the sugars they contain. But we do not have enzymes that can digest cellulose. So this plant material passes through the whole digestive tract unchanged. Nutrition specialists call it **dietary fiber**, or roughage.

By the time digested food reaches the end of the ileum, the last part of the small intestine, the protein, carbohydrate, and fat nutrients have been absorbed into the bloodstream. But there are still some valuable minerals and a lot of water that need to be recycled. They are absorbed in the large intestine. This part of the digestive tract is actually much shorter than the small intestine—only about 6 feet (close to 2 meters) long. It is called the *large* intestine because it is much wider—2 to 3 inches (about 5 to 8 centimeters) in diameter, which is more than twice as wide as the small intestine.

The ileum merges with the large intestine in the lower right part of the abdomen, at a T-shaped joint. One arm of the T forms a short pouch called the **cecum**, from which hangs a finger-shaped structure called the **appendix**. In humans the cecum does not seem to do anything useful (and the appendix sometimes causes trouble by getting infected so badly that it must be removed surgically). In animals such as rabbits, however, the cecum provides a home for bacteria that digest cellulose into useful nutrients.

The large intestine has two main parts. The first is the **colon**, which goes up the right side, bends to run sideways across the top of the abdominal cavity, and then turns downward and back, in an S-shaped curve, to

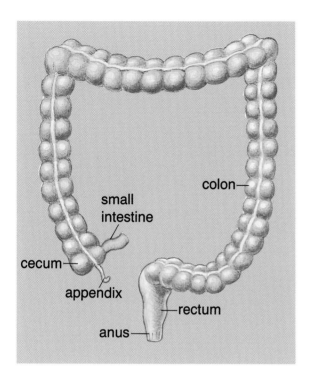

small
intestine

colon—

cecum—

appendix

—rectum

anus—

connect with the second part, the **rectum**. This is a fairly straight, 5-inch (about 13-centimeter) tube that leads to the anus, an opening to the outside. A powerful sphincter muscle holds the end of the rectum closed.

As the remains of the digested food move through the large intestine, more than 90 percent of the water is absorbed through the intestinal wall, along with various minerals. Did you know that you have your very own colony of bacteria living inside your colon, feeding on the waste products of your food? These bacteria are called the **microflora**. They do not usually cause harm; some of them even produce vitamins that your body can use. But the action of the bacteria on food wastes produces gas bubbles, which may make embarrassing noises or cause pain when they stretch the intestinal walls.

As the wastes lose water moving through the colon, they are shaped into soft masses called feces. The feces are about three-fourths water. About 30 percent of the solid part is dietary fiber, and another 30 percent is made up of the bodies of dead bacteria. The brown color comes from the remains of worn-out red blood cells. You get rid of about 3 to 5 ounces of feces each day (or up to a pound if your diet contains a lot of fiber).

Peristaltic contractions move the feces along. When feces enter the rectum you feel an urge to defecate. In babies the sphincter guarding the anus then opens automatically. But gradually the young child learns to control the anal sphincter muscle, keeping it closed when an urge comes at an inconvenient time.

WHAT HAPPENS TO YOUR LUNCH

L et's follow what happens when you eat a meal—for example, a tuna salad sandwich with lettuce on whole wheat bread, a glass of milk, and an apple for dessert.

Your mouth is already watering when you take the first bite out of the sandwich. Saliva mixes with the food as you chew, and an enzyme, salivary amylase, begins to break down some of the starch in the bread. Soon your tongue and teeth have shaped the mouthful into a soft bolus. With a shove from your tongue the bolus enters your pharynx and slides down your esophagus.

Smelling the food, thinking about eating, and then chewing the first mouthful have already started your stomach secreting gastric juice. So the bolus plunges into an acid bath that softens the food and begins to digest the protein in the tuna. But carbohydrate digestion stops as the acid seeps into the food because the salivary enzyme cannot work in acid. Swallows of milk, more bites of the sandwich, and then chunks of apple follow that first mouthful. Soon your stomach has plumped out from its skinny J shape. Its walls contract rhythmically, mixing and churning the food into a soupy liquid. After a while, small portions of this chyme are squirting through the pyloric sphincter into the duodenum.

Hormones and nerve messages have prepared for the next stage of digestion. Cells in the intestinal lining and in the pancreas have been pouring out digestive juices. The acid from the stomach is neutralized, and new enzymes go to work. The proteins from the tuna, bread, and milk are split into their amino acid building blocks. Carbohydrates from the bread, milk, and apple are split into simple sugars. The gallbladder has sent bile into the duodenum to work on the fats from the milk and the mayonnaise in the tuna salad. The bile breaks the fat into tiny droplets, which are digested by enzymes into the fat building blocks, fatty acids and glycerol. Peristaltic contractions continue to mix and churn the food materials and move them along.

Tiny villi in the lining of the small intestine absorb the digested nutrients into the blood and lymph systems. Most of them find their way to the liver, where some are stored and others are chemically changed.

Meanwhile, the cellulose from the bread, lettuce, and apple, along with other waste products, is still moving along, into the large intestine. The soft, soupy mass gradually thickens as water and minerals are absorbed and bacteria feed on the wastes. Finally, solid feces move into the rectum and you feel an urge to defecate.

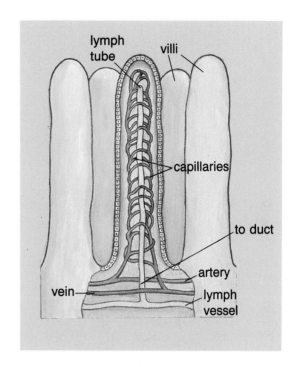

TIMETABLE OF DIGESTION

0 hours: You start to eat.

1/2 hour: Your stomach is full.

2 hours: Chyme is entering the duodenum.

6 hours: Your stomach is nearly empty.

12 hours: Nutrients are being absorbed in the small intestine.

18 hours: Wastes are forming in the large intestine.

24 hours: Feces are ready to leave the body.

SECTION 5

A BALANCED DIET

If you could eat anything you wanted, what would you choose? How about ice cream, cake, and candy at every meal, with potato chips for snacks and plenty of soft drinks to wash them down? Meals like those might seem like a treat at first, but you would soon grow tired of them—and your body would not stay healthy very long. For good health you need a variety of foods, providing enough of all the important nutrients: proteins, carbohydrates, fats, vitamins, minerals, and water.

Proteins are needed for their building materials: amino acids for your body to build into its own proteins. These help to form body structures. The enzymes that run the body's chemical reactions are also proteins, and so are many of the hormone messengers. Meat, fish, poultry, dairy products, beans, and nuts are good protein-supplying foods.

Carbohydrates are the body's ready energy sources. They are supplied mainly by foods from plants, such as fruits, vegetables, and the grains in cereals and breads. Milk also contains a carbohydrate called lactose.

Fats provide a backup energy source and also are important parts of nerves and some hormones. Butter and margarine are almost pure fat; so are salad and cooking oils. Meat contains a lot of fat, even if you cut away the fat you can see; so do dairy products, unless they are specially processed to remove part or all of their natural fats.

Vitamins play important parts in the body's chemical reactions. So do minerals, and some of them also help to build body structures, such as the calcium in teeth and bones. Foods such as fruits and vegetables, bread and cereals, meat, fish, and dairy products contain various vitamins and minerals. But highly processed "junk foods" such as candies and soft drinks may contain little of these valuable nutrients.

You lose a lot of water each day, in your urine, feces, and sweat, and all this water must be replaced. It seems obvious that milk and juices contain a lot of water. But solid foods such as fruits, vegetables, and meat also contribute to the water in the diet.

Dietary fiber, found in fruits, vegetables, and whole grains, is not really a nutrient since your body cannot digest it. But a good diet should include fiber, too, to help keep things moving along in the digestive tract.

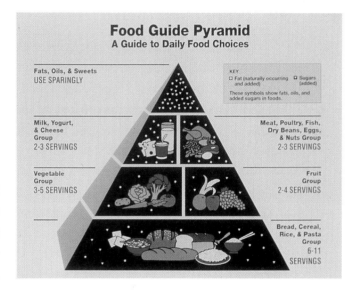

The USDA developed this diagram to show recommended daily servings of major food groups.

A healthy diet includes all the nutrients and fiber, in the right proportions. You need protein, but if you eat too much of it, your body may have trouble getting rid of its harmful waste products. You need some fat, but too much will make you overweight. Even vitamins and minerals may be harmful if you take in too much of them.

Nutrition experts recommend eating a balanced diet, selecting foods according to a "nutrition pyramid" developed by the U.S. Department of Agriculture. The balanced diet should include large amounts of fruits, vegetables, and grains, smaller amounts of high-protein foods like meats and nuts (many of which also supply fats), and only a little of the very fatty or sugary foods like butter and ice cream. This healthy diet will consist of about 15 percent protein, 55 percent carbohydrate, and no more than 30 percent fats.

EATING TOO MUCH

Have you ever worried about your weight? Surveys have shown that up to 90 percent of Americans think they weigh too much and would like to lose at least 15 pounds. One study found that 50 percent of nine-year-old girls were dieting. Most of the people worrying about their weight are not really overweight, but **obesity** is a big problem in the United States and other industrial countries. Nutrition experts say that one-fifth to one-quarter of Americans weigh at least 20 percent more than they should.

Obesity is more than just an image problem. Overweight people are more likely to suffer from heart disease, diabetes, and other serious health problems.

People get fat by eating more nutrients than their bodies can use. Just why this happens is not so clear. Some nutritionists believe that obesity is caused by hereditary defects in the way the body regulates the appetite and uses food. That may be why diets rarely work. A number of people are unable to stick to a diet that may be very boring or leaves them feeling hungry all the time. Other people lose weight on a diet but then gain it right back as soon as they start eating normally again.

The experts say that the only effective way to lose weight is to eat a balanced diet and cut down on the total amount of food (especially foods high in fats). The dieter should eat enough to feel satisfied and aim to lose weight very gradually, a little at a time. Exercise can help in a weight-loss

---

DID YOU KNOW . . .

The average adult in the United States eats more than half a ton of food each year.

*Regular exercise helps keep the body healthy and
is an important part of weight control.*

program by using up nutrients and also stepping up the rate of the body reactions that generate energy.

It is hard not to feel a little worried about your weight when each day you see pictures of fashion models and entertainers who are extremely thin. A number of people—especially young people who are not very confident about themselves yet—may compare themselves to these artificial ideals and feel ugly and inadequate. Some become so obsessed with their weight that they develop serious eating disorders.

Today many young people suffer from **anorexia nervosa**. They keep on dieting even after they become underweight. When they look in the mirror, they still think they look fat, and they cut down on the food they eat even more. Eventually they may become very ill.

In another eating disorder, **bulimia**, the person goes on food binges, eating huge amounts of food, and then vomits or uses laxatives to get rid of the nutrients. The bulimic may keep at a normal weight, but the constant bingeing and purging upsets the body systems and leads to illness.

The treatment of eating disorders is a long, complicated process. Supervised eating programs are combined with counseling to work out the person's emotional problems. Recently doctors have found that a drug, Prozac, can help to stop a bulimic's urge to binge on food.

NOT ENOUGH FOOD

While people in the United States and other developed nations suffer from "diseases" of affluence, such as obesity and heart disease, in many parts of the world the problem is too little food rather than too much. Each day, about 35,000 people starve to death. Many more suffer from **malnutrition**, the lack of enough food (or the right foods) to eat.

In some places, such as North Africa, there is very little rain. Some years there is not enough water for food crops to grow. Widespread famines may also be caused by bad storms and floods that wash away the crops and soil, or by wars that prevent people from growing their crops.

When people do not get enough to eat, their bodies do not have a supply of nutrients for growth and repair. To get energy for breathing, moving, and other activities, they use up their stored fats and even begin to digest the proteins from their muscles. They become very thin and tired and cannot fight off disease germs the way well-nourished people can. The children suffer most, because their growing bodies need plenty of protein and other nutrients.

Even people who seem to be eating a lot of food may suffer from malnutrition if they are not getting enough of the right kinds of foods. In many places, for example, people eat mainly grains and other foods high in carbohydrates but low in proteins. Some food crops, such as corn or rice, do not contain enough of all the amino acids that are needed to make human proteins. Children may become weak and ill after they stop drinking their mother's milk, and their mental development may slow down.

A lack of vitamins or minerals can also make people ill. Old-time sailors used to suffer from bleeding gums and weak bones during long sea voyages. Some even died from this condition, which was called **scurvy**. They lived on a diet of hard biscuits and salted meat. In the 1700s it was dis-

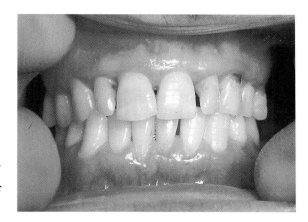

Scurvy is a disease caused by a lack of vitamin C. It can result in bleeding gums and weakened bones.

covered that drinking lime juice or eating lemons or limes could prevent scurvy. We know now that these fruits contain an important nutrient, vitamin C.

A lack of vitamin A, found in carrots, broccoli, and various other foods, can cause night blindness and skin problems. Vitamin D, supplied by fish and fortified milk, is especially important for growing children because it helps the bones to grow strong and straight. B vitamins, found in whole grains, are needed for the health of the brain and nerves. People who eat only white bread or polished rice may not get enough of these nutrients because the outer husks of the grains, which contain most of the vitamins and minerals, are stripped off during processing. The mineral calcium is needed to keep the bones strong, and iron is used by the body to build new red blood cells.

When we see pictures of starving children in Somalia or some other famine-stricken country, we want to help feed them. But emergency food shipments only help for a little while. The people also need help in getting enough water, seeds, and equipment to produce food for themselves. Organizations such as Oxfam America are helping to fight hunger all around the world.

FOOD POISONING

We eat foods to provide the nutrients we need. But sometimes the foods we eat may make us ill. Some common foods can be poisonous. When potatoes are green they contain a poison that can cause nausea and vomiting. Some wild mushrooms contain deadly poisons. Clams and other shellfish may be contaminated with poisons from polluted water or from the bodies of the water creatures on which they feed.

The most common cause of food poisoning, though, is bacteria. Food manufacturers use various methods to keep our foods free of harmful

A scientist for the Food and Drug Administration works with salmonella cultures in a regular food testing program. Salmonella are bacteria that cause food poisoning.

germs or to prevent them from multiplying. Milk is pasteurized (heated to a very high temperature, then rapidly cooled) to kill bacteria. Deep freezing and drying foods prevent the growth of germs. Canned foods can stay wholesome for a long time because most bacteria cannot grow and multiply without air. (An exception is a very deadly bacterium that causes botulism. It does grow without air, but it is killed by the heat and high pressures of the canning process.)

Bacteria may get into foods during packing, shipping, or preparation. Perhaps someone who handles the food has not been careful to wash after going to the bathroom. Flies spread disease germs as they crawl over garbage or animal feces and then land on uncovered food.

A technician checks a catch of shrimp for possible contamination from polluted waters.

Some bacteria make poisons as they grow in food. Others cause damage to the digestive tract after they have been eaten. Either kind can make you sick. The most unpleasant symptoms of food poisoning, **vomiting** and **diarrhea**, are actually results of the body's efforts to protect itself.

Vomiting results when the poisons in spoiled foods irritate the stomach and duodenum and set off a powerful reaction. Messages to the vomiting center in the brain are relayed back along nerves to the digestive tract. The cardiac sphincter relaxes to open the way from the stomach to the esophagus, and the abdominal muscles and diaphragm contract violently, squeezing the stomach so that its contents spurt upward, out through the esophagus. Later the pyloric sphincter may also relax, permitting material from the duodenum to be vomited out. (That is why vomiting may leave you with a taste of bile.) The vomiting center can also be stimulated by pain, motion sickness, or strong emotions.

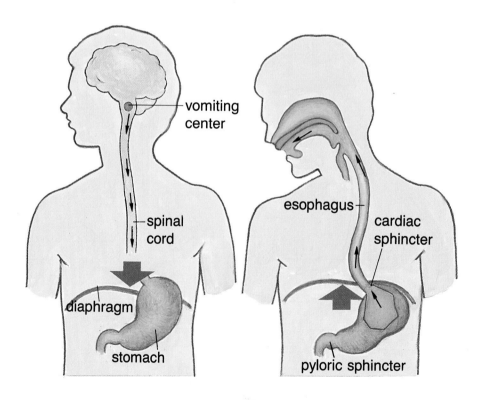

Diarrhea occurs when bacterial poisons from spoiled foods irritate the delicate lining of the intestines. Peristaltic contractions become strong and rapid, causing painful cramps and sweeping the intestinal contents along. There is not enough time for solid feces to form, and the stools are soft and watery. Diarrhea gets bacteria and their poisons out of the body quickly, but it can have harmful effects. Some nutrients are lost because the food was not completely digested and absorbed. And a lot of water is lost, too. If diarrhea continues for a long time, the body can become dangerously dehydrated. So drinking a lot of liquids to replace the lost body fluids is an important part of the treatment for food poisoning and diarrhea.

WHEN THINGS GO WRONG

"Excuse me," you say automatically when you burp or belch. You may feel even more embarrassed when gas emerges (sometimes noisily) from the other end of the digestive tract. These may be normal side effects of digestion, but when they occur often they may be signs of a problem.

Nearly everyone suffers now and then from indigestion, or **dyspepsia**, a feeling of discomfort or pain in the abdomen, sometimes accompanied by nausea. Perhaps you ate too much, or ate so fast that you swallowed a lot of air, and your stomach is too full. Digesting foods such as beans and cabbage may produce a lot of gas. Very spicy foods like curry or chili and drugs such as alcohol or aspirin can irritate the lining of the digestive tract. Emotional upsets can make the stomach secrete too much acid. Bacterial or viral infections can also cause irritation and pain.

Many people take **antacids** to neutralize the stomach acid when they are suffering from indigestion. These medications may relieve discomfort or it may get better by itself.

Peptic ulcers are a more serious problem: open sores that form in the stomach and duodenum when there is not enough mucus to protect the delicate lining cells from the stomach acid. Ulcers produce a burning pain in the upper abdomen, heartburn, and nausea. Emotional stress, which increases acid secretion and decreases mucus secretion, may help to cause ulcers. Some scientists believe a bacterial infection may be involved. Drugs that decrease acid secretion can help peptic ulcers to heal.

Many people take medications for bowel problems, such as diarrhea and **constipation** (a failure to defecate regularly). Some people have diarrhea after eating dairy products because they can no longer digest the milk sugar lactose. Constipation can result from often ignoring the urge to defecate. Too much water is absorbed in the large intestine, the feces become dry and hard, and defecation may be painful. Regularly taking **laxatives** (drugs that stimulate defecation) can actually cause constipation by stopping the normal body reflexes.

Irritable bowel syndrome (IBS) is a chronic disorder of the colon. People with IBS experience abdominal pain, gas, bloating, constipation or diarrhea, or both. Doctors are not sure exactly what causes IBS. But proper diet, stress management, and medication can help to reduce symptoms.

Sometimes indigestion, nausea, and abdominal pains may be symptoms of more serious problems, especially when there is blood in the stools or the person is losing weight. Cancer, a disease in which body cells suddenly begin to multiply uncontrollably, spreading into other tissues and forming masses called **tumors**, can occur in any part of the digestive tract, from the mouth down to the colon and rectum. Cancer may be treated with drugs, radiation, or by surgery to remove the tumor.

Raw or undercooked beef, pork, or fish may contain **parasites** such as tapeworms, which settle down in the intestines and feed on the nutrients there. Anchored by suckers on its head, a tapeworm can grow up to 30 feet (9 meters) long. Tiny pinworms are a common problem in children. They live in the large intestine and cause itching when they come out through the anus to lay their eggs. Scratching the itch may get the tiny worm eggs under a child's fingernails, and they may get on clothes, bedding, and toilet seats. People who touch these things may pick up eggs, then may touch their mouths. Pinworm eggs that are swallowed travel down to the intestines, where they grow into a new generation of pinworms.

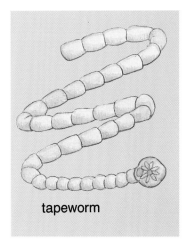

tapeworm

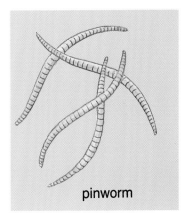

pinworm

SEEING A DOCTOR

Most people with digestive disorders never bother to go to the doctor. They just treat themselves, changing their diet to avoid foods that "disagree" with them and taking over-the-counter medications such as antacids for indigestion and laxatives for constipation. Americans spend more than a billion dollars each year for nonprescription drugs for digestive problems.

But when a digestive problem goes on for a long time, when pain is very severe, or when blood is found in vomit or stools, it is a good idea to consult a doctor. Many middle-aged and elderly people have regular check-ups including tests for digestive system problems because the most serious ones, such as ulcers and cancer, can be treated more effectively when they are found early, before they have had much time to develop.

Doctors today have a number of ways to look at the digestive tract. One approach is the **GI series**, a series of X rays showing the organs of the upper and lower digestive tract. (GI stands for "*gastro*intestinal.") The digestive organs are made of soft tissues and normally would not show up on an X ray. So the patient swallows a flavored "milkshake" containing the chemical **barium sulfate**. Barium is somewhat similar to the mineral calcium that forms the structure of bones, and like calcium it shows up very well on X rays. So as the swallowed barium sulfate moves from the mouth down the esophagus into the stomach and then the duodenum, it outlines each digestive organ in turn. To see the organs of the lower digestive tract, barium sulfate is introduced in the form of an **enema**, a liquid that is forced in through the anus and flows up into the rectum and colon, outlining them and showing up tumors and other abnormalities.

There are also instruments that allow a doctor to actually look into the digestive tract and even snip off bits of tissue for testing. The **endoscope** is

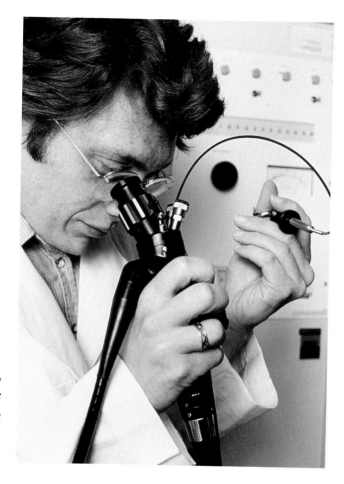

Using an endoscope, the doctor can see the insides of the esophagus, stomach, and duodenum.

a long, flexible tube, containing glass fibers that transmit light. It is inserted through the mouth and threaded down the esophagus into the stomach and duodenum. Tools for looking at the lower digestive tract include the **proctoscope,** which shows only the rectum, and the **sigmoidoscope**, which goes up into the S-shaped part of the colon.

Special dyes may be swallowed or injected to make the liver and gallbladder visible on X rays. Some high-tech tools can also be used to get information about the digestive organs. Ultrasonograms produce a picture of the organs by plotting the reflections of bouncing waves of ultrasound (sound too high-pitched for our ears to detect). CAT scanners give an X-ray picture of a whole "slice" of the body. MRI scanners form a similar picture by the effects of radio waves.

FOOD FOR THE FUTURE

A person from the nineteenth century might have a hard time recognizing some of the foods you can buy in a supermarket today. Fresh fruits and vegetables are shipped around the world and are available any season of the year. Flour and grains are sold in neat packages instead of open bins, and people buy cereals, baked goods, and even whole dinners already prepared. Just add water, or pop a tray into a microwave oven, and you are ready to eat. There is a confusing variety of choices—different brands, different kinds of foods, even ethnic dishes like spaghetti, chow mein, or knishes.

Will the future bring new foods and eating habits that we would find just as bewildering? We can speculate on what some of the future trends in foods will be on the basis of things that are happening today.

The world's population is growing, which means that we will need more food to feed everyone. Agricultural scientists are working to improve food crops, and they are using some new scientific tools and techniques. They have learned how to grow whole plants from leaf or stem cells, and to transfer genes—the hereditary chemical instructions—from one cell to another. Scientists are using genetic engineering to produce tomatoes that ripen naturally during shipping, corn with a more complete protein, and frost-resistant food plants that can grow in more parts of the world. They have transferred genes to cows that allow them to produce more milk and are trying to supply wheat and other grain crops with genes from legumes like peas and beans, which can grow without needing added nitrogen fertilizer.

As medical scientists learn more about the causes of heart disease and other serious illnesses, people have become concerned about too much cholesterol and saturated fats in the diet. The food industry is producing leaner meats and various meat substitutes. Some of them are based on soybean proteins, with artificial flavors and other additives that make them taste almost like the original meats. Health-conscious people are also eating more vegetables, which are less fattening and contain vitamins and other chemicals that seem to protect us against diseases.

There will probably be more emphasis on food from fish in the future, too. Two-thirds of our planet is covered by water, and yet less than 2 percent of the food we eat comes from the seas. Some recent studies have suggested that chemicals in fish oils can help to protect our health. Researchers are developing new methods for fish farming and for converting fish wastes into nourishing, high-protein products.

As the earth's population continues to grow, fish farming will help answer the increased demand for food.

Astronauts on long space voyages may make much of their food from algae—single-celled plants—grown in big vats of nutrient liquid and then processed to add pleasing textures and flavors. "Single-celled protein" foods may become more common on earth, too, as the world's food needs increase.

GLOSSARY

acinus—one of the structures in the pancreas that produce digestive secretions. (Plural: acini.)

amylase—a starch-digesting enzyme.

anorexia nervosa—an eating disorder in which the person diets obsessively.

antacids—chemicals taken to neutralize excess stomach acid.

anus—the opening at the end of the gut.

appendix—a fingerlike structure that hangs from the cecum.

barium sulfate—a salt that is taken to coat the lining of the digestive tract and make it visible in X rays.

bile—a substance secreted by the liver and stored temporarily in the gallbladder; it aids in fat digestion by breaking down large globs of fat into tiny droplets on which digestive enzymes can act.

bolus—the soft ball of food formed in the mouth after chewing and swallowed into the esophagus.

brush border—the microvilli.

bulimia—an eating disorder in which the person periodically goes on food binges, then takes laxatives or induces vomiting to get rid of the excess food before it can be digested.

canines—the pointed teeth to each side of the incisors; eyeteeth.

cardiac sphincter—the ring of muscle surrounding the opening from the esophagus into the stomach.

carnivore—an animal that eats only (or mainly) other animals.

cecum—a pouchlike structure at the junction of the small and large intestines.

cellulose—an indigestible food chemical made of many sugar molecules linked together; the major component of dietary fiber.

cholecystokinin—a hormone secreted by the duodenum, which stimulates the pancreas to secrete digestive juices and causes the gallbladder to contract, sending bile into the small intestine.

chyme—the soupy liquid into which food is converted in the stomach.

chymotrypsin—a protein-digesting enzyme of the pancreas.

colon—the first part of the large intestine.

constipation—a failure to defecate (have bowel movements) regularly.

dentin—the yellow, bonelike layer of teeth below the enamel.

diarrhea—frequent soft or liquid bowel movements, accompanied by intestinal cramps.

dietary fiber—indigestible plant material contained in foods.

digestion—the conversion of food to smaller chemical components that the body can use for energy or building materials.

digestive tract—the sequence of tubular structures through which food passes while being converted to nutrients and waste products; includes the mouth, esophagus, stomach, small and large intestines.

duodenum—the first part of the small intestine.

dyspepsia—a feeling of discomfort or pain in the abdomen after eating; indigestion.

emulsifying agent—a substance that breaks down fat globules into tiny droplets that can stay suspended in water.

enamel—the hard, whitish covering of teeth.

endocrine gland—a gland whose secretions pass into the bloodstream and are carried by blood to their site of action.

endoscope—a long tube containing a fiberoptic probe permitting a doctor to see the inside of the digestive tract and perform surgery.

enema—the introduction of a liquid into the digestive tract through the anus.

enzyme—a protein that helps other chemicals to react; digestive enzymes aid in breaking down foods in the body.

epiglottis—a flap of tissue in the pharynx that closes the opening into the trachea during swallowing.

esophagus—a muscular tube that leads from the mouth cavity to the stomach.

exocrine gland—a gland whose secretions are delivered by tubular ducts.

feces—body wastes (undigested food matter plus intestinal bacteria) formed in the large intestine.

food chain—an interrelationship of living organisms, each feeding on others farther down the chain.

gastric juice—the mixture of stomach digestive secretions.

gastrin—a hormone secreted by the stomach, which stimulate cells in the stomach lining to produce hydrochloric acid.

GI series—a series of X rays showing the organs of the gastrointestinal (digestive) tract.

glucagon—a hormone produced in the pancreas that causes sugar to be released from the glycogen stores in the liver, resulting in a rise in the amount of glucose in the blood.

glycogen—animal starch; an energy-storage chemical made up of thousands of glucose units.

gullet—the esophagus.

gut—the digestive tract.

hard palate—the front part of the roof of the mouth.

heartburn—pain felt in the front of the chest due to splashing of stomach acid up into the esophagus.

Heimlich maneuver—a first-aid remedy for choking due to a food particle caught in the trachea.

herbivore—an animal that eats only plant materials.

hormones—chemical messengers that help to control and coordinate body activities.

hydrochloric acid—a strong acid, produced by glands in the stomach.

hypothalamus—a portion of the brain containing control centers for various body functions, including hunger.

ileum—the last section of the small intestine.

incisors—the chisel-shaped front teeth, specialized for cutting.

insulin—a hormone produced in the pancreas that causes sugar to be stored in the liver, resulting in a drop in the amount in the blood.

intestinal juice—digestive secretions of the intestinal lining (including mucus, sodium bicarbonate, and digestive enzymes).

irritable bowel syndrome (IBS)—a chronic disorder of the colon.

islets of Langerhans—structures in the pancreas that produce insulin.

jejunum—the middle section of the small intestine.

lacteal—a lymph vessel inside a villus, into which digested fats are absorbed.

large intestine—the tubular portion of the digestive tract that follows the small intestine; includes the colon and rectum; most of the absorption of water occurs here.

laxative—a drug taken to stimulate defecation.

lipase—a fat-digesting enzyme.

liver—an organ that secretes bile, which helps in fat digestion; it also stores sugar in the form of glycogen and performs numerous other functions including the detoxification of poisons.

lobules—subdivisions of the liver.

malnutrition—the lack of enough food (or the right kinds of foods).

microflora—bacteria, yeasts, and other microorganisms that normally live on or in the human body.

microvilli—tiny projections on the surface of the villi.

molars—broad, three-cusped teeth at the back of the jaws; also called tricuspids; specialized for crushing and grinding food.

mucosa—the innermost layer of the gut.

mucus—a thick, slippery liquid that coats the inside of the gut.

nutrient—a food chemical.

obesity—overweight.

omnivore—an animal that eats both plant and animal foods.

organic materials—the chemicals of living organisms; all contain the element carbon.

pancreas—an organ that secretes digestive enzymes; it also has endocrine functions, secreting several hormones that regulate the body's use of sugar.

pancreatic duct—tube leading from the pancreas into the duodenum.

pancreatic juice—the mixture of digestive secretions produced by the pancreas and secreted into the duodenum.

papillae—the "bumps" on the surface of the tongue that contain taste buds.

parasite—an organism that lives on or in the body of another organism, sharing its nutrients.

parotid glands—salivary glands just below the ears.

pepsinogen—a stomach secretion that is changed into the protein-digesting enzyme pepsin.

peptic ulcers—open sores in the lining of the stomach or duodenum.

peristalsis—wavelike contractions of smooth muscles that move the contents of tubular organs along (for example, in the digestive system).

pharynx—the common passageway in the throat leading from the nose and mouth cavity to the trachea (air pipe) and esophagus (food pipe).

portal vein—a blood vessel that carries digestive products from the small intestine to the liver.

premolars—two-cusped teeth that follow the canines; also called bicuspids; modified for crushing and grinding food.

proctoscope—a tool for looking at the rectum.

pulp—the soft center of a tooth, containing blood vessels and nerves.

pyloric sphincter—the ring of muscle surrounding the exit from the stomach into the intestines.

rectum—the last part of the large intestine.

rennin—a milk-digesting enzyme produced in the stomachs of children.

rugae—soft folds formed by the inner walls of the empty stomach.

saliva—fluid secreted by glands in the mouth; it contains starch-digesting enzymes and also helps to soften and moisten food.

salivary glands—three pairs of glands in the mouth that secrete saliva.

scurvy—a disease caused by a lack of vitamin C in the diet.

secretin—a hormone secreted by the jejunum, which stimulates the intestinal lining to secrete digestive juices.

serosa—the outermost layer of the gut.

sigmoidoscope—a tool for looking at the rectum and the S-shaped part of the colon.

small intestine—the tubular portion of the digestive tract leading from the stomach; includes the duodenum, jejunum, and ileum; the major work of digestion and absorption occurs here.

sodium bicarbonate—a salt that neutralizes stomach acid in the chyme entering the intestines.

soft palate—the part of the roof of the mouth toward the back.

stomach—a baglike organ in which food is churned and mixed; acid and digesting enzymes begin the digestion of protein.

sublingual glands—salivary glands located under the tongue.

submaxillary glands—salivary glands in the lower jaw.

submucosa—the sturdy, elastic layer that gives the gut its shape.

taste buds—sensory receptors for tastes.

teeth—hard, bonelike structures in the mouth, used for biting and chewing food (the preliminary stage of digestion).

trypsin—a protein-digesting enzyme of the pancreas.

tumor—a swelling caused by a sudden growth of cells. Malignant, or cancerous, tumors grow uncontrollably; benign tumors stop growing and do not spread.

uvula—the U-shaped flap of tissue that hangs down at the back of the soft palate and closes off the airway leading to the nose during swallowing.

vagus nerve—the main nerve involved in the work of the digestive system.

villus—fingerlike projections from the inner surface of the small intestine, through which nutrients are absorbed into the bloodstream. (Plural: villi.)

vomiting—a violent expulsion of food from the stomach back out through the esophagus and mouth.

TIMELINE

1570   Ancient Egyptian physicians had treatments for stomach and intestinal worms, and used suppositories to introduce drugs into the bowel.

300   Theophilus of Chalcedon (Greek) dissected animals and humans and described the liver, pancreas, and bile ducts.

160   Galen (Greek) thought food was carried from the gut to the liver, where it was changed into blood.

A.D.

1672   Reinier de Graaf (Dutch) collected pancreatic juice.

1700s   René de Réaumur (French) showed that birds' stomach juices help to break down food; Lazzaro Spallanzani (Italian) showed that digestion is not the same as fermentation or decay and that the stomach secretes digestive juices.

1753   James Lind (Scottish) used citrus fruits to cure scurvy (a disease caused by a lack of vitamin C) in sailors.

1824   William Prout (English) showed that hydrochloric acid was present in the stomach.

1833   William Beaumont (American) reported on his experiments on digestion in a soldier with a hole into his stomach; he demonstrated that alcohol inflames the stomach lining.

1835   Theodor Schwann (German) identified the enzyme pepsin in stomach juice; later he showed that bile emulsifies fats.

late 1800s   Richard Kühne (Austrian) isolated the enzyme trypsin in pancreatic juice.

1902   Ernest Starling and William Bayliss (English) discovered secretin, the hormone that stimulates secretion of pancreatic juice.

1904   Ivan Pavlov (Russian) won a Nobel Prize for experiments on digestive secretions and the effects of conditioned reflexes.

1915   "Typhoid Mary" (American), a cook, was identified as the source of typhoid fever outbreaks in the New York City area.

1982   Barry Marshall (in Australia) discovered a bacterium, *Helicobacter pylori*, in the digestive tracts of ulcer patients and suggested it was the cause of ulcers.

1980s   New, far more effective antiulcer drugs (cimetidine, ranitidine, famotidine, misoprostol) were developed.

1993   Studies showed that antibiotic treatments for *H. pylori* in addition to standard antiulcer drugs were much more effective in curing and preventing ulcers.

1993-1994   Several genes involved in the development of colon cancer were discovered.

INDEX